CLAIRE EAMER

LIZARDS
IN THE
SKY

ANIMALS
WHERE YOU LEAST
EXPECT THEM

annick press
toronto + new york + vancouver

Text © 2010 Claire Eamer

Annick Press Ltd.

Edited and copyedited by Elizabeth McLean
Proofread by Tanya Trafford
Cover and interior design by Irvin Cheung / iCheung Design, inc.
Cover photographs: (flying lizard) Stephen Dalton / First Light; (leaves) www.istockphoto.com; (back cover illustrations) from *Alice's Adventures in Wonderland and Through the Looking Glass.* Original illustrations by Sir John Tenniel, scans © istockphoto.com / Darren Hendley

We acknowledge the support of the Canada Council for the Arts, the Ontario Arts Council, and the Government of Canada through the Book Publishing Industry Development Program (BPIDP) for our publishing activities.

 ONTARIO ARTS COUNCIL
CONSEIL DES ARTS DE L'ONTARIO

Cataloging in Publication
Eamer, Claire, 1947-
    Lizards in the sky : animals where you least expect them / by Claire Eamer.

Includes bibliographical references and index.
ISBN 978-1-55451-264-5 (pbk.).—ISBN 978-1-55451-265-2 (bound)

    1. Animals—Adaptation—Juvenile literature. I. Title.

QL49.E245 2010   j591.4   C2010-901326-3

Printed and bound in China

Published in the U.S.A. by
Annick Press (U.S.) Ltd.

Distributed in Canada by
Firefly Books Ltd.
66 Leek Crescent
Richmond Hill, ON
L4B 1H1

Distributed in the U.S.A. by
Firefly Books (U.S.) Inc.
P.O. Box 1338
Ellicott Station
Buffalo, NY 14205

Visit our website at **www.annickpress.com**

To the family biologists,
Joan and Ted, who sparked my
fascination and still feed it.

CONTENTS

FANCY MEETING YOU HERE!

IMAGINE SITTING ON A LOG and staring down into a fresh, clear stream. What might you expect to see? Maybe a duck paddling on the surface. Or a frog sticking its nose out of calm water near the bank. And fish. You'd certainly hope to see fish darting through their underwater world with the flip of a tail, snatching bits of food out of the current or prowling the river bottom in search of smaller creatures to eat.

You wouldn't expect to see a little bird poking its sharp beak between the stones at the bottom of the stream. You probably wouldn't expect to see a spider inside a silk home. Or an animal that looks like a miniature deer, cruising in the watery shadows beneath the stream bank. But you might be surprised.

To air-breathers like us, the underwater world is as alien as the moon or Mars. We swim clumsily, frightening the fish. Without a supply of air, we can't spend more than a couple of minutes below the surface. We can't set up house there, or prepare a meal, or raise a family. But a few air-breathing animals have found surprising ways to live, forage, hunt, or hide in the world of the fish.

In fact, all over Earth—in water, on land, in the air, and even in the darkest depths of land and sea—creatures have discovered how to live in the most unexpected places.

A PLACE to CALL HOME

EARTH IS OUR HOME, but we can't live in every part of it—at least, not without a lot of help. Like other species of animals and plants, we need a specific set of conditions in order to survive, let alone live comfortably.

If you were plunked down on Earth with no more protection than shorts and a T-shirt, where could you live?

To begin with, in most parts of the planet, you'd probably need more clothes, either to protect you from the cold or shade you from the sun and heat. Both heat and cold can kill, so you'd be safest in a warm climate—but not too warm.

In 1983, in Vostok Station, Antarctica, the temperature dropped to -89.2°C (-128.6°F), the coldest ever recorded.

Breathing is another limitation. Human lungs aren't designed to absorb oxygen from water, so that rules out the three-quarters of the globe covered by water. You'd need to live on land, where you can breathe air. However, you still need to drink, so you'd want a good supply of fresh water.

And then there's the problem of food. You would definitely want something to eat—not once in a while, but day after day.

So…maybe a nice, sunny orchard with year-round fruit, a clear stream running through it, and a snug den for the cool of the night? That might work. But there aren't many places like that.

Humans, of course, live in far more areas of Earth than our imaginary orchard. Tools and technology keep us comfortable in regions that are too cold, too hot, too dry, or too wet. Adjusting our behavior helps too. People who live in very hot places usually stay out of the sun during the hottest part of the day. People who live in very cold places wear layers of clothing to stay warm. We can even live and travel underwater for months at a time—with the help of complicated and expensive technology, such as submarines.

Humans can't survive very cold places without insulation, such as warm clothing.

ANIMAL ADVENTURERS

ANIMALS, TOO, CAN ADAPT. They build dens and nests for shelter and protection. They grow thick fur coats or fluff out their feathers in the cold. They retreat to shady or cool places in the heat. Some animals migrate, traveling as much as halfway around the world each year to find the right conditions for survival.

A few animals have taken adaptation even further. They are pioneers, moving into environments that would kill most of their relatives, environments that normally belong to entirely different kinds of animals. Instead of dying, they've found ways to thrive.

These animal pioneers have solved the basic problems of breathing, moving, eating, and reproducing in a hostile environment. But how can a fish move on land? How can a snake fly? How can a frog survive in a desert? How can a worm live in ice?

An arctic fox is cozy in the cold with its thick coat of white fur.

This rainbow trout doesn't need strong bones because the water supports its weight.

NOT ALL BONES are EQUAL

FISH GOTTA SWIM, birds gotta fly.... That's a line from an old song— and it sounds true, doesn't it? After all, fish come equipped for swimming and birds are built for flying. What else would they do?

But some fish live on shore, some birds walk, and some four-footed mammals swim or even fly. They've managed to make bodies built for one way of life work in another.

Fish, birds, and mammals have bodies designed for specific purposes. They're all vertebrates—animals with backbones. They all have heads, brains, eyes, skeletons, and similar sets of internal organs. But those basic parts can be very different.

Consider, for example, fish bones. They're thin and fairly bendy, and really annoying when you try to pick them out of your supper. They can afford to be relatively weak, because they don't have to support the fish's weight. Water takes care of that. The fish simply

Cows and birds are both vertebrates, but their bones are very different.

floats underwater, propelling itself by flexing powerful muscles along its sides.

Chicken bones aren't nearly as annoying on your dinner plate as fish bones. They're bigger and easier to see, and they don't bend. That's because a chicken isn't held up by water. Instead, it has a skeleton of rigid bones to support its body.

But weigh the chicken bone in your hand. Not very heavy, is it? If you break it open, you'll find that the bone is just a hollow tube with a bit of soft tissue inside. Most birds, even poor fliers like chickens, have lightweight bones to make flying easier.

Cattle don't fly, so they don't need light bones. Instead, they need bones strong enough to support a heavy animal. If you look inside a steak bone, you'll see that it's solid most of the way through. It doesn't bend, and it doesn't break easily.

Fish bones, bird bones, and mammal bones are as different as bones can be, but they suit the lives most of those animals lead. If a fish, a bird, or a mammal tries to live a different kind of life, it will need to make changes. Sometimes a change in behavior is enough, but other changes go bone-deep.

> Birds use their hollow bones to store fresh air for breathing.

MOVING OUT of the ORCHARD

SO WHY DO ANIMALS go to all that trouble? For the same reason humans move to regions like the icy Arctic, or the high Andes mountains, or the dry Sahara Desert—to find a place to live.

Our imaginary orchard with year-round fruit would be great, but it would fill up quickly with other people and animals. Meat-eaters—predators—would show up, hoping to make a meal of the fruit-eaters. Soon, it would be a crowded, dangerous place with too little food and nowhere to hide.

The solution is to move where there's enough food and fewer predators, and where it's safe to bring up the babies. In order to survive in your new home—whether you're human or animal—you'll probably have to make a few changes to your behavior or your body, or both.

And that's exactly what the animals in this book have done.

1 BRAVING THE WAVES

⌒ LIVING in WATER ⌒

SURVIVING IN WATER isn't easy for animals whose ancestors were designed for a different environment. For one thing, how do you breathe? Fish get oxygen from water, but birds, reptiles, mammals, and many other creatures need to breathe air.

And how do you stay warm? Water conducts heat away from your body much faster than air does. Warm-blooded animals, such as birds and mammals, need to keep their body temperatures within a narrow range in order to survive. Most insects and reptiles have lower body temperatures, but even they will die if they get too cold.

Another problem can be what to do with the kids. Most newborn or newly hatched offspring of air-breathers also breathe air. How can parents make sure their offspring have what they need to live?

This dog's fluffy coat was meant for life on land. In the water, it doesn't do much to keep the dog warm.

⤏ DIPPING and DIVING ⤎

IF YOU'RE A GOOD SWIMMER, people say you swim like a fish. They never say you swim like a bird. But consider the penguin. These odd birds can't fly at all, but when they dive beneath the ocean's surface and flap their flipper-like wings, they wheel and soar underwater as gracefully as any bird in the sky.

Penguins look like water animals, but other birds are deceptive. Take, for example, the American dipper.

It's the middle of winter in the mountains of northwestern Canada. Snow blankets the land, and ice covers lakes and rivers. But a soft gurgle comes from a patch of open water where a stream rushes too quickly to freeze. A small, gray-brown bird, about the size of a starling, perches on a lip of ice, peering into the fast-moving current and bobbing up and down. Then it dives straight into the icy water and disappears. A few seconds later, it pops to the surface with a fish clamped in its sharp beak.

An American dipper is perfectly comfortable sticking its head in the stream to watch for underwater prey.

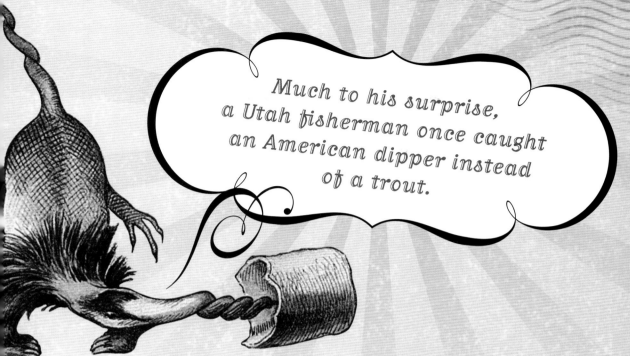

Much to his surprise, a Utah fisherman once caught an American dipper instead of a trout.

The American dipper is an underwater hunter found almost everywhere in North and South America. Using its short, broad wings, it flies through the water to the stream bottom in search of fish and insect larvae. By pumping its wings and gripping stones with its long toes, the dipper can stay down for as long as 15 seconds. That doesn't sound long—but imagine holding your breath and, at the same time, running as hard as you can. Suddenly, 15 seconds seems much longer.

Although the dipper looks like a fairly ordinary bird, it has some clever adaptations. Flaps close over its nostrils when it dives, and transparent membranes slide across its eyes so that it can see underwater. An extra-thick downy undercoat keeps the dipper warm, and waterproof oil from a large gland above its tail keeps it dry. Its blood can even hold extra oxygen for its underwater hunting expeditions.

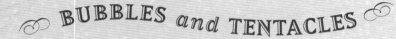

BUBBLES and TENTACLES

MANY ANIMALS THAT HAVE ADAPTED to unusual conditions still appear quite normal. But the star-nosed mole is just plain weird! If you look at a star-nosed mole from the front, you see an oversized pair of digging claws on either side of 22 naked tentacles, arranged around its nose like a fleshy pink flower. You can barely see the eyes of the chipmunk-sized mole behind the mask of tentacles. But that doesn't matter to the mole because it can barely see. It doesn't need to.

The star-nosed mole spends its life in the dark, underground or underwater, in the wetlands of eastern Canada and the United States. It hunts worms and insects by feel, using its wriggling tentacles, which contain 25,000 super-sensitive touch receptors that feed information to the mole's brain. As soon as the tentacles encounter a worm or insect, the mole acts. It gulps its prey down in less time than it takes a driver to slam on the brakes at a red light. This strange-looking creature may be the fast-food champion of mammals.

But that's not its only special talent. The star-nosed mole can smell food underwater—by blowing bubbles.

Cozy under a coat of waterproof black fur, the mole scrabbles along the marsh bottom, gently blowing bubbles out of its nostrils and sucking them back before they break. The air bubbles pick up traces of scent from whatever they touch, and the mole's brain sorts out food scents from rock and mud. Star-nosed moles are so good at bubble-sniffing that they can follow the trail of a worm or a fish, even through the smelly mud of a wetland.

The tentacles on the star-nosed mole's nose help it smell and feel in water as well as on land.

✑ CASTLE *in the* WEEDS ✑

AMERICAN DIPPERS AND STAR-NOSED MOLES are visitors to the watery world, but the water spider lives there full-time. It's born underwater, hunts underwater, and spends its whole life underwater—even though it needs air to breathe.

You can find water spiders in shallow, cool wetlands from Britain eastward across Europe and northern Asia. Watch for a small, silvery creature swimming on its back among the marsh plants. The silver is actually tiny bubbles of air trapped in the dense hairs of the spider's underside—an air supply it can carry with it wherever it goes.

The water spider lives in a home of silk and air. It spins a waterproof silken net and anchors the net to plants near the surface. Then it ferries air bubbles from the surface down to its net. It shakes the bubbles off its belly hairs and goes back for more until the air

A shimmery bubble in the underwater grasses is home to a water spider.

Water spider mothers take care of their babies for four weeks before launching them into their watery world.

makes its silk house balloon up like an old-fashioned diving bell (a large, air-filled dome that divers used before the invention of scuba gear)—which is why the water spider is sometimes called the diving-bell spider. Water spiders spend most of the day inside their homes. At night, they hunt underwater larvae and surface-dwelling insects such as water striders.

The female water spider builds an extra-large home with a special chamber at the top for her eggs. The baby spiders hatch there, into a silvery world completely surrounded by water. Eventually, carrying personal air supplies on their abdomens, they head off to build their own silken nests. They'll make brief visits to the surface to grab some air, but otherwise the underwater world is the only one they'll ever know.

SURFING the SURFACE TENSION

OUT ON THE OPEN OCEAN, small air-breathers such as insects are extremely rare. According to scientific estimates, at least a million species of insects exist on Earth, but only five species—all closely related—live at sea, far from land.

Sea skaters can stand and walk on the water's surface without getting wet.

They're sea skaters, cousins of the water striders you see tip-toeing across the surface of a freshwater pond. All five sea-going species have bodies just about long enough to stretch across the eraser end of a pencil. Like all insects, they have six pairs of legs. The front pair is fairly short, but the middle and back pairs are long and thin, like jointed stilts that stick out sideways from the insect's body. Those stilt legs support sea skaters on the most fragile of habitats—the surface tension of the open ocean, mainly in warm, tropical regions.

Surface tension results from the attraction between water mole-cules—which makes them cling together enough to be a liquid. Their clingy-ness is strong enough to provide a home for a wide variety of small animals. Some creatures live underwater, dangling from the surface tension. Others, such as sea skaters, live on top.

Sea skaters can move around on the surface without break-ing through into the water below, their long legs spreading the insect's weight over more area, like little snowshoes on snow. If they do break through, they have a sort of built-in life jacket. Their bodies are covered by dense layers of hairs. If a sea skater is pushed beneath the water, bubbles trapped in the hairs will pop it to the surface, where it clambers back up and grooms itself dry.

What can an insect at sea find to eat? Tiny animals and larvae drifting at the top of the ocean make a good meal for a sea skater. So do larger things, such as small fish, fish eggs, and even jellyfish.

When she's ready to lay eggs, a female sea skater attaches them to floating debris, and the baby sea skaters hatch at sea, already fit to skitter across the fragile surface of the water. They will probably live their entire lives there, never seeing or touching land.

A leaf is as big as a raft to a water strider.

SLITHERY SWIMMERS

SEAGOING INSECTS ARE SURPRISING, but how about seagoing snakes? And not just a few snakes. In 1932, sailors in the Strait of Malacca near Malaysia came across millions of snakes clustered together, so many that they made a line about as wide as a road lane and 100 kilometers (over 60 miles) long.

Sea snakes are actually quite common in the tropical waters of the Pacific and Indian oceans, but most species live close to shore or near coral reefs where they can find plenty of food. Only one species, the yellow-bellied sea snake, ventures far out on the open ocean, drifting on the warm currents. It can be found from the east

Yellow-bellied sea snakes spend their entire lives in water.

coast of Africa all the way to warm waters off the Pacific coast of Central America and Mexico. Often, the snakes will gather in large numbers—like the cluster of snakes in the Strait of Malacca—where there's a good source of food.

As snakes go, the yellow-bellied sea snake isn't big—on average, just long enough to stretch across a doorway. It has a yellow underside, black back, and a spotted, paddle-like tail that helps it move smoothly through the water. On land, though, it's helpless. The snake's yellow belly is smooth and V-shaped, rather than round—great for swimming, but terrible for gripping the ground and moving on land.

Not that there's much chance of meeting a yellow-bellied sea snake out of water. The snakes are born at sea and live there all their lives.

Most sea snakes, like this one, live in shallow water near the shore, but the yellow-bellied sea snake lives in the open ocean.

> The venom of the beaked sea snake of the South Pacific is so powerful that one drop can kill three grown men.

And that's lucky for land-dwellers. Like all sea snakes, the yellow-bellied sea snake is descended from cobras, but its venom is even more deadly than a cobra's. However, with a small mouth and fangs, it isn't equipped to bite people.

Yellow-bellied sea snakes eat fish, but they don't spend energy hunting them. They simply float on the sea surface, often close to seaweed and debris. Smaller fish are attracted to floating things, because the creatures they eat tend to gather nearby. So the snake hangs about, looking like a floating stick, until a fish comes close. Then it whips its head to the side, snagging the fish with its sharp teeth and swallowing it whole, head-first.

Yellow-bellied sea snakes have some useful abilities for life in the sea. They can dive as deep as 50 meters (165 feet) and are able to stay down for over an hour by absorbing oxygen through their skin. They can swim both backward and forward. And they can tie themselves in knots.

Knot-tying doesn't sound useful until you realize that most other snakes rub their bodies against hard surfaces to get rid of parasites and to help shed their old skin when they molt. Of course, in the open ocean there are no hard surfaces. The yellow-bellied sea snake has an answer. It loops itself into a knot and runs the knot from one end of its body to the other, scraping its skin clean or peeling off old skin.

A DIVING DEER

What is the last animal you might expect to find at the bottom of a stream? How about something that looks like a deer, but is the size of a fox, with an oddly mouselike face—and fangs? That's the chevrotain (SHEV-ruh-tane).

There are about ten species of chevrotain, also called mouse-deer, ranging from cat-sized to fox-sized. Most live in the forests of Asia, from India to Indonesia, with the largest in central Africa. They have stocky bodies, thin legs, and large upper canine teeth that sometimes stick down outside the jaw like tusks. Although they look more or less like deer, chevrotains are something else entirely. They're Tragulids, members of a family that split off from the ancestors of today's deer, cattle, goats, sheep, and antelope about 50 million years ago.

At least three species of chevrotain are surprisingly good swimmers, one from Africa and two from Asia. The African chevrotain, when threatened, often dives into water to escape. It creeps along the stream bottom with its nose pointed down to avoid being swept upward by the current. If the predator is still there when it paddles to the surface to take a breath, the chevrotain will dive right back under.

In Borneo, researchers watched one little chevrotain dive and resurface for over an hour, staying down for more than five minutes at a time.

Chevrotains spend most of their time on land, but they're almost as comfortable in water.

2 HIGH AND FAIRLY DRY

∽ LIVING on LAND ∾

AS HUMANS, we're comfortable with life on land. Our bodies are designed for it. We have legs for walking, lungs for breathing, and skin that protects our delicate internal organs from drying out.

For some animals, land is desperately dangerous. Fish flop helplessly, unable to breathe or move themselves back to the water. A bird with a damaged wing is easy prey for hunters. A stranded jellyfish, exposed to the air, shrivels and quickly dies.

But there are exceptions—fish that spend more time on land than in water, birds that never leave the ground, and former water-dwellers that have moved entirely onto land. How do they deal with the problems of breathing, moving, eating, and escaping danger?

Jellyfish are mostly water and can't survive long on land.

NATURE'S GARBAGE DISPOSAL

IF YOU PRY A ROCK LOOSE from damp soil, you'll often find startled, buglike creatures underneath—small and gray-brown, with lots of segments and even more legs. You can find the same animals in rotting logs, under garden planters, and even in dark, damp corners of basements, skittering away from the light and attention.

For such drab creatures, they have a lot of names. In different parts of the world, they're called sow bugs, pill bugs, woodlice, roly-polies, potato bugs, slaters, and more. They look like insects with too many legs, but they aren't even closely related to insects. They're isopods, part of a large group of animals called crustaceans. Their relatives include barnacles, water fleas, and such tasty treats as lobsters, crabs, and shrimp.

Most crustaceans are water-dwellers. Only a few of the isopods have moved onto land full-time, but the land-dwellers are a big success. There are thousands of species of woodlouse, and you can find them around the world.

Woodlice have seven bands of tough, armor-like material across their backs, and seven pairs of legs attached to their undersides. They eat things that are dead and decaying, and even their own poop. They're so good at disposing of natural garbage that some researchers use them to clean tissue off the bones of dead animals.

Although they've been landlubbers for millions of years, woodlice still have gills that extract oxygen from water. However, they carry the water around with them. Their gills are tucked beneath their abdomens in waterproof compartments that keep them moist. Some woodlice also have tubes or cavities that work like lungs, passing oxygen directly into the

blood. To avoid drying out, they stick to dark, damp places. Some species can roll into a tight ball, which helps to protect them from predators and also stops moisture from evaporating through their undersides. Some can even suck water into their bodies through tubes in their anuses.

Water-dwelling isopods lay eggs that hatch into floating larvae. The female woodlouse has developed a trick to keep her larvae safe and wet on land—a kind of pouch on her underside that's full of water. She lays her eggs into the pouch, where the male fertilizes them. As many as 200 microscopic larvae hatch and swim around inside her pouch. In a few days, they emerge into the world as miniatures of their parents, ready to strike out on their own.

Eels can wriggle out of the water, but they have to stay wet.

∽ IT CAME *from the* SWAMP! ∽

IT SOUNDS LIKE A HORROR MOVIE. A beetle ambles along the muddy shore of an African swamp, minding its own business. Suddenly a giant, snakelike form rises from the water and a huge mouth descends, enveloping the helpless beetle. The terrifying monster slides back into the swamp, taking the beetle down to its death.

Of course, the snakelike animal, the eel catfish, is a giant only to a beetle. It's actually about as long as a hammer. It's a distant relative of the bewhiskered catfish you might find in a home aquarium, eating fish-food leftovers from the gravel. And even though it hunts on land, the eel catfish never completely leaves the water.

However, real eels sometimes do crawl out of the swamps and rivers they live in, around much of the world. Eels may look like snakes, but they are fish and they absorb oxygen from water, either through gills or directly through their skin. As long as their skin stays damp, they can venture onto land. An eel out of water might be migrating, leaving a stream that's drying up, or just looking for a new food supply.

On rainy nights or overcast days, freshwater eels can sometimes be found wriggling through wet grass or over damp ground, heading to another body of water, sometimes a few hours' travel away. Their snaky wriggle is so effective that they can even climb the steep sides of dams and waterfalls. But if the sun comes out before they complete their journey, it will dry their skin so they can't breathe—and they will die.

SKIPPING between LAND and SEA

BREATHING IS NO PROBLEM for mudskippers—and they also get around fine on land. These little fish, most no longer than your hand, skitter around the warm, muddy shorelines of oceans bordering Africa, Asia, and Australia. They have googly eyes, big mouths, and look a bit like cartoon fish.

Mudskippers have adapted so well to the world of air that they spend most of their time out of water. They dip into shallow pools to avoid drying out, and dart into air-filled burrows at the first sign of trouble. As their name suggests, mudskippers hop nimbly across boot-swallowing mud at low tide, using their tails and a muscular set of fins that look remarkably like front legs. Their fins are so strong that mudskippers can clamber over mangrove tree roots or even climb them to avoid the oncoming tide.

A mudskipper perches on the wall of its burrow for a good view of the mudflats.

Three mudskippers line up on a rope, out of the water and safe from big, hungry fish.

Wait… What's a fish doing hiding from the tide in a tree? It happens to be a safe place to hide from predatory fish that come in with the tides. And mudskippers are quite content in a tree. They have gills that absorb oxygen from water. But they can also breathe air through special, oxygen-transferring cells in their gills and through their skin, as long as it stays moist.

Most fish have eyes designed to see underwater, but the mudskipper has solved that problem too. Its bulgy eyes stick up from the top of its head, more like frog eyes than fish eyes. To keep the eyes moist, skin folds beneath each eye form cups that hold water. When its eyes start to dry out, the mudskipper retracts them quickly into the cups to moisten them, then slides them back into place.

Mudskippers have also figured out what to do with the kids—or, in fish terms, the eggs. Fish normally lay eggs in water, but mudskippers aren't normal fish. First, the male mudskipper uses his fins to dig out a large chamber in his burrow. Then he sets out to entice a female to join him, sometimes with a sort of dance that involves puffing out his cheeks, arching his back, and even flipping his body into the air. If a female is suitably impressed, she wriggles into the burrow and deposits her eggs on the roof and upper walls of the chamber.

In some species, both parents care for the eggs, and in others, only the male does. Egg care includes guarding the burrow and keeping it full of fresh air. While the tide is low, mudskippers carry fresh, oxygen-filled air into the burrow in their mouths, so that both the parent fish and the eggs they guard can wait out the high tide in comfort.

The mudskipper digs its burrow with its mouth, adding each mouthful of mud to the wall around its territory.

❧ THE BIRD in the BASEMENT ❧

BURROWS DOT THE DRY GROUND of the prairie too. Lots of them. Most are home, as you might expect, to rodents such as ground squirrels and prairie dogs. But if you're lucky, you might spot something a bit more surprising—an owl, with white eyebrows and startling yellow eyes, that sticks its head up from a hole and checks for danger before climbing out and flying off.

The burrowing owl lives in prairies, deserts, and open spaces from South America to southern Canada. It has even been spotted at Florida golf courses and airports. It's small for an owl, not much bigger than a robin, with mottled sandy-brown feathers that blend into the brown of dry grass and low shrubs. Still, it's unmistakably an owl, with a round owl head, a fierce beak, and the claws of a hunter.

Most owls nest in trees, where they're safer from predators and can watch for passing mice and other tasty morsels. But there aren't many trees in the burrowing owl's territory. Instead, there are holes in the ground, so many that the owls don't need to dig their own burrows. They just take over the abandoned burrow of a prairie dog or ground squirrel and modify it to suit their needs.

Male burrowing owls are enthusiastic home decorators. They often collect dried manure from large mammals and scatter it throughout their burrows. Researchers had suspected that they might be trying to disguise the scent of baby owls from predators such as badgers and coyotes. However, a study in the United States showed that the smelly floor covering makes no difference to predators. It does, however, appear to tell other owls that the burrow is already occupied. And it attracts insects and other creatures that burrowing owls are happy to eat.

A burrowing owl checks for danger before carrying its prize, a mouse, into its underground home.

PEDESTRIANS with WINGS

SOME BIRDS HAVE GIVEN UP flight entirely and live their whole lives on the ground. Ostriches and emus are so well adapted to that kind of life that it's hard to imagine them flying. But others look as if they ought to fly. Take, for example, the kakapo, the world's biggest parrot.

The kakapo lives on several of New Zealand's offshore islands. Almost goose-sized, it's a bright, mottled green, with a whiskery face. Long ago, the kakapo was probably a normal, flying parrot. But for millions of years, New Zealand had no ground-based predators that the kakapo needed to fly away from, so it gave up flying entirely and grew larger. Now, it travels everywhere on foot, walking along tree branches or trudging through forest undergrowth on its large feet, with its head forward and its body parallel to the ground as if always in a hurry.

Kakapo wander the forest floor at night, looking for tasty berries and plants.

Kakapo are so heavy that their wings do little more than slow them down when they jump from a branch.

Kakapo roost in thick vegetation or in natural crevices during the day and come out at night to feed. Totally vegetarian, they'll eat most things the forest has to offer, but they're particularly fond of pollen and fruit. And just because they walk doesn't mean kakapo are slow. They can put on a burst of speed when they need to and cover considerable distances. Scientists reported that one kakapo traveled 5 kilometers (3 miles) in a night, pausing to feed along the way.

When the male is ready to mate, he climbs through the forest to a high ridge or outcrop above the trees. There he settles into a hollow in the ground and sends out a low-pitched booming call that echoes over the surrounding forest, letting female kakapo know that it's time to meet him. When several males are calling at the same time, it's said to sound like distant thunder.

Life on the ground isn't always easy, even for an extra-large parrot. In fact, there are no kakapo left on the New Zealand mainland. When humans arrived in New Zealand, probably less than a thousand years ago, they brought cats, rats, and other predators that ate the kakapo's eggs and killed their young. The last few birds were moved to an island with no predators, where they're being helped back from the edge of extinction. There are more kakapo now than there were a few years ago, but not enough to assure the survival of the species.

The whiskery-faced kakapo is the largest parrot in the world.

FISH IN A LOG

While slogging through a swampy seashore forest in Belize, in Central America, researchers accidentally kicked open a rotting log above the waterline. To their surprise, a tiny fish, no longer than your finger, tumbled out, flipping and wiggling. It was a mangrove killifish, a creature that lives in the shallow ponds around mangrove roots, along the Atlantic coast from Florida to northern Brazil. When the ponds dry up, the fish move to any bit of water they can find, including puddles in broken coconut shells and discarded beer cans. But inside logs?

When the researchers examined the log, they found a hundred of the little fish in its cracks and hollows. Since then, more log-dwelling killifish have been found, sometimes in tunnels bored through logs by insects. Dozens of them may fill a single narrow tunnel, lined up end to end.

They may be waiting for the rainy season and the return of their favorite ponds, but scientists aren't sure why mangrove killifish leave the water. They seem to be comfortable in the air, though. Fish have been seen at night, flipping out of the water to capture insects and then flipping back in.

In the damp air inside logs, mangrove killifish can survive for months. They appear to breathe and excrete waste through their skin, and their gills grow thicker. When they're ready to leave their logs, they wriggle out, tumble into the water, and go back to living like fish.

A mangrove killifish can live out of water for months, often hiding in the cracks of damp logs.

3 HARD, HARD GROUND

LIVING in a DESERT

LIVING IN A PLACE as dry as a desert is hard, really hard. The main problems are lack of water and extreme temperatures, both hot and cold.

We tend to think of deserts as hot and sandy, but they aren't all like that. One of the driest places on Earth is the Ross Desert, a frozen expanse in Antarctica, where no moisture has fallen for 2 million years or more.

The Gobi Desert is hard, dry earth and rock, more like the usual idea of a desert, but it's deep in the cold heart of northern Asia. Frigid winds sweep across it, and temperatures can drop to -40 degrees.

And in Africa's Sahara Desert, the largest desert outside the polar regions, the air temperature regularly goes above 50°C (122°F) and the ground temperature can climb to 70°C (158°F) or higher.

You'd expect to find a camel in the desert, but some of this camel's neighbors are surprising.

In all these places—in fact, in all deserts, hot or cold—lack of water is a huge problem. Living things can't survive without it. But in cold deserts, moisture is locked up in ice and snow. And in hot deserts, water evaporates quickly into the air.

LIVING in the FAST LANE

DESERTS ARE DRY. That's what makes them deserts. But even in a desert, rain sometimes falls. And when it does, unexpected things happen. Brown, dead-looking plants turn green, flowers bloom, and shrimp come out to play.

Shrimp? In 1955, in the Mojave Desert in the southwestern United States, rain fell and flooded Bicycle Dry Lake for the first time in 25 years. Within hours, the water was cloudy with fairy shrimp and other tiny crustaceans, hatched from eggs that had lain in the dry lake bottom for a quarter of a century.

Fairy shrimp eggs are sometimes sold in toy and science stores, where they're called sea monkeys. If you put them in a bit of salty

Fairy shrimp are delicate and almost transparent, but their eggs are tough enough to survive in the desert for years.

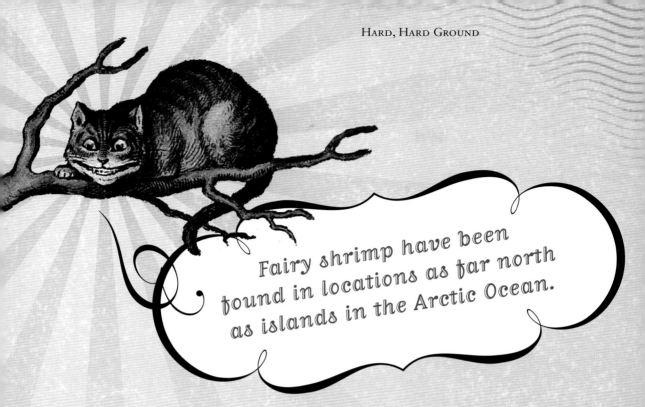

Fairy shrimp have been found in locations as far north as islands in the Arctic Ocean.

water, they'll hatch within hours. After all, surviving a few months in a sealed packet is no challenge compared to years in the desert. And fairy shrimp are so good at surviving that they're found in most regions of the world.

In the warm, shallow pools that linger in the desert after a rain, the eggs hatch and the shrimp thrive. They rush through their life cycle at breakneck speed because there's no time to waste. Every day, as the sun's heat sucks the moisture back into the air and the pools shrink, the hatchling shrimp swim around on their backs, eating decaying organic matter and growing quickly.

Within a couple of weeks, they're adult shrimp, almost transparent with large, dark eyes. Depending on the species, they have up to 19 pairs of paddle-shaped legs to propel them around their evaporating pond. Before the water disappears completely, they'll lay and fertilize the eggs that will produce a new generation of fairy shrimp when rain falls again.

PACKING WATER to GO

IT'S NOT ONLY TINY CREATURES such as shrimp that wait for rare desert rain. If you dug down about a spade's length into the hard, dry clay of the southern Australian desert—and if you dug in the right spot—you'd find a large, bloated, brownish-green frog tucked inside a cocoon and sunk into a sort of coma.

What you've found is a water-holding frog, waiting for rain. It can wait like that for months. The cocoon, made from its own shed skin, is almost waterproof and stops the frog from losing moisture. And water-holding frogs have plenty to lose. They can absorb water through their skins and store it in their cells and in an extra-large bladder, so when they retreat underground at the end of the rainy season, they're full of liquid.

Water-holding frogs peek out of the mud that will protect them until the next rainy season.

Once the frogs are settled in their cocoons, their body processes slow down in a kind of hibernation that reduces the amount of water they need to survive. When heavy rains arrive at the beginning of the rainy season, they wake up. But by then the ground is rock hard, so they have to wait until moisture seeps down to turn the clay to mud. Then the frogs scramble up to the surface and set about the important business of reproducing.

Like fairy shrimp, water-holding frogs have to move fast to produce the next generation. The females deposit hundreds of eggs into temporary pools and swamps on the desert surface. The tadpoles develop quickly, and by the time the rains stop and the pools turn to mud, they're ready to retreat underground.

The young water-holding frogs dig their way backward into the soft clay. They keep digging, scooping away mud with their hind feet and sinking ever lower beneath the surface until they're deep enough to wait out the dry season. And there they stay, gradually building up a protective cocoon of shed skin as they wait month after month for the return of the rains.

DADDY DELIVERS a DRINK

BIRDS CAN'T WAIT OUT dry times the way shrimp and frogs can. They need both food and water year-round. For the Namaqua sandgrouse of the Kalahari and Namib deserts of southern Africa, those two things aren't often in the same place.

Sandgrouse are sandy-brown, pigeon-like birds that live in dry regions of Africa, Asia, and southern Europe. They survive by eating the seeds of desert plants, which may grow far from a water source. The birds spend their days pecking at the hard ground, consuming thousands of seeds. Every two or three days, the sandgrouse have to fly off for a drink.

Now, good waterholes are rare in the desert, especially where the Namaqua sandgrouse live. Each morning, sandgrouse from a large area fly to the same waterhole. They arrive alone or in small flocks, but by a couple of hours after sunrise, several thousand may be crowded around, jostling each other as they scoop up water and gulp it down. Once their thirst is quenched, they fly back to their feeding grounds. For some birds, this expedition involves a round trip of 80 kilometers (50 miles).

That's a hard journey for an adult, and impossible for a chick. However, sandgrouse have found an ingenious answer to the question of how to raise the kids in a desert. Daddy delivers the water.

On their bellies, male sandgrouse have special feathers that suck up water like a sponge. During the early weeks when their chicks are too young to fly, the males have an extra chore. Once they've drunk their fill at the waterhole, the male sandgrouse wade in and soak their bellies until the feathers have absorbed as much water as they can hold. Then they fly back over the desert to where their chicks are pecking up seeds. When the male lands, the chicks rush over and drink the water from their father's belly feathers. Each young bird can take in a third of its own weight in water, enough to tide it over until Daddy delivers the next drink.

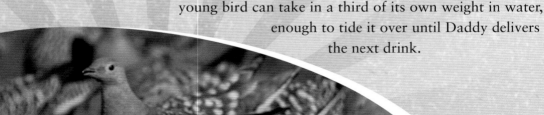

Sandgrouse enjoy the water after a long, dry flight over the desert.

BEATING the HEAT

LACK OF WATER isn't the only problem desert-dwellers face. Temperature extremes are also a challenge, especially for mammals. A mammal needs to keep its body temperature within a narrow range. A few degrees too low or too high, and the body begins to shut down. If body temperature isn't corrected, the animal will die.

So why is the white-tailed antelope ground squirrel, a furry rodent with a bushy tail, scurrying around the hot deserts of the southwestern United States and northern Mexico in the heat of the day? Other rodents, such as kangaroo rats, are active at night when it's cool, and retreat to burrows during the day.

The antelope ground squirrel has some advantages over most mammals when it comes to handling extreme temperatures. Its normal body temperature is close to ours, but it can survive moderate changes much more easily than we can. It can even go into a state called torpor, much like hibernation, if the temperature drops too low in winter.

But it doesn't rely only on its body's ability to withstand heat and cold. Although it forages for food during the day, this squirrel is most active when it's cooler, in morning and late afternoon. During the hottest hours, it dashes from shade patch to shade patch, where it stops briefly to nibble on seeds or fruit or gulp down a passing insect. Or it climbs into a bush, away

The white-tailed antelope ground squirrel nibbles all day, even in the heat of the desert sun.

from the hot ground. The antelope ground squirrel can even create its own patch of shade by curving its bushy white tail over its body like a parasol.

If it's still too hot, the little squirrel ducks into one of its many burrows. By sprawling with its belly flat against the cool earth, it can lower its body temperature by more than a degree a minute.

And if even more cooling down is needed, the squirrel has one more weapon in its heat-fighting arsenal. Most larger mammals sweat or pant to cool themselves off, but not this animal. It drools. The squirrel then spreads the saliva over its neck and chest. It's a bit like sticking your head under a tap on a hot day. As the water evaporates, it sucks some of the heat from your body. The antelope ground squirrel's trick sounds messy, but it works!

SLOW and STEADY isn't ALWAYS BEST

WOULD YOU BE SURPRISED to find a tortoise in a desert? Although tortoises do live on land, when you think about it, desert life doesn't seem like such a hot idea for these creatures.

For one thing, tortoises are reptiles and, like all reptiles, their body heat is determined by their surroundings. Like mammals, though, their body temperature has to stay within a specific range. Above or below that range, they become inactive and eventually die. In deserts, the temperature can be dangerously hot during the day for a tortoise stuck inside a heat-absorbing shell.

Tortoises are too slow and clumsy for the temperature-control techniques used by other reptiles. Snakes and lizards solve temperature problems by

A desert tortoise will even pee on itself to cool off.

moving. They bask in the morning sun to warm up, then spend the rest of the day avoiding the heat by burrowing underground, climbing off the ground, or opening their mouths wide so that evaporating saliva can cool their bodies.

Tortoises—especially the large, clumsy desert tortoise of the Mexican and southwest American deserts—can't dart off in search of shade, most of them burrow very slowly, and they're terrible at climbing. However, the desert tortoise is an expert at using evaporation to cool off. It produces frothy saliva that increases the amount of heat it can lose by letting its mouth gape open. And if that's not enough, desert tortoises pee on themselves. As the urine evaporates, it carries more heat away from their bodies. The tortoise even has an extra-large bladder, perhaps to carry a good supply of cooling pee.

Lizards, like other reptiles, use the heat of the sun to warm their bodies.

A MAMMAL THAT LIVES LIKE AN ANT

Who could possibly expect an animal like the naked mole rat? It's a blind, hairless rodent, with wrinkly skin and buckteeth that would make a beaver proud. About the size of a gerbil, it lives beneath the dry, sun-baked earth of eastern Africa. Its large colonies are organized like ant colonies. A single female, the queen mole rat, produces all the colony's babies, while the rest of the colony takes care of her and them. A queen mole rat can produce more than a thousand pups in her lifetime.

For most of the year, the land is so dry that there's little to eat on the surface, so mole rats have adapted to living underground. They dig tunnels in the hard ground with those giant buckteeth, searching for roots and tubers. Above ground, the desert's plants might look dead, but below ground, their roots are chock-full of nutrients and water.

Mole rats don't need to see, since they're always in the dark, but they do need to smell, feel, and hear. They feel their way along the tunnels with long whiskers and identify food by its smell. When a naked mole rat finds a prize tuber, it bites off a piece and rushes back to the rest of the family, chirping in triumph. The sound, and the smell of the fresh tuber, tell the other mole rats all they need to know.

Naked mole rats protect themselves from the desert heat by living underground.

4 HIGH IN THE SKY

✦ LIVING *in* AIR ✦

THE AIR ISN'T NEARLY as crowded with animals as the land and sea. There are birds, winged insects, and even a few winged mammals, but most of the time you can look toward the sky and see nothing and no one looking back at you. There are reasons for that.

For one thing, flying is hard work. You need strong muscles and lots of energy. At the same time, you have to be very light. Humans aren't designed for flight, even if we could grow wings. We have heavy bones to support our weight on the ground, and when we build up our muscles we just get heavier.

Second, there really isn't much need for most animals to fly. Usually animals live close to everything they require—food, shelter, and a suitable place to reproduce. If they have to move with the seasons, walking or swimming takes a lot less energy than flying.

Still, there are ways to take to the air without wing-flapping, and some unexpected animals have found this out.

Wouldn't you love to fly like a bird? Or maybe even like a lizard?

49

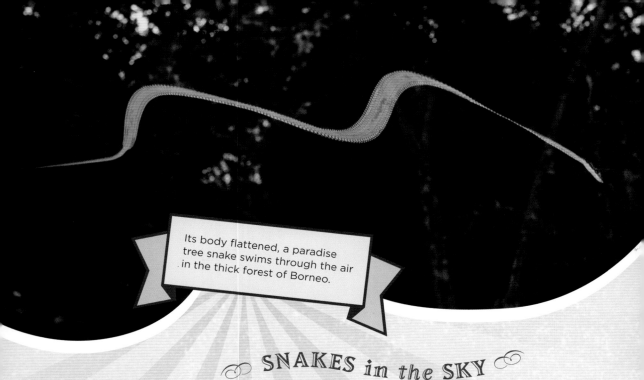

Its body flattened, a paradise tree snake swims through the air in the thick forest of Borneo.

∽ SNAKES in the SKY ∽

YOU EXPECT TO SEE BIRDS and bees in the air, but snakes? It sounds like a great idea for a scary movie. But if you're in the forests of Borneo or Malaysia—at the right moment—you might spot a bright yellow-green snake, flat as a ribbon, passing overhead.

There are five related species of flying snake, all living in the thick forests of Singapore, Thailand, Malaysia, Indonesia, or Borneo. They're not active fliers like birds or insects that flap their wings to rise into the air. Flying snakes have no wings to flap. Instead, they climb into the forest canopy and launch themselves from a tree branch.

Flying snakes spend most of their time high in the forest, slithering along branches in search of lizards and other tree-dwelling prey. Like all snakes, they're as skinny as a piece of rope. They certainly don't look like fliers. But snakes can do unusual things with their bodies. Their ribs aren't attached to anything on the belly side, and some snakes can spread their ribs to the sides and change their body shape. Flying snakes use their rib-spreading abilities to fly.

The best flier is the paradise tree snake, which grows to about a meter (3 feet) long. It has yellow-green scales with dark edging, almost jewel-like, and sometimes red markings on its back.

When it wants to fly, a paradise tree snake slithers to the end of a branch and dangles down, hanging by its tail with its head curved upward in the shape of the letter J. Then it whips its body up, straightens it, and pushes away from the branch.

As its tail releases the branch, the snake spreads its ribs and flattens its body. Slightly hollowed on its belly side now, it's about twice as wide as normal and shaped like a narrow parasail. At the same time, the snake pulls its head and tail toward the center of its body to form an S shape.

For the first part of the flight, the snake falls through the air, gaining speed as it drops. The faster it goes, the more lift it gains, just as an airplane goes faster and faster down the runway until it has enough lift to take off. Once the snake has enough lift, it can fly and even steer. It undulates back and forth, swimming through the air as it would in water. With slight movements of its tail or body, it can change direction in midflight. And when it lands, on another branch or on the ground, the snake simply pulls in its ribs to make its body round again and slithers away.

It may not sound like an effective way to fly, but it works. One paradise tree snake had a recorded flight of 21 meters (69 feet). That would take it across a five-lane highway with room to spare.

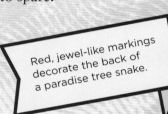

Red, jewel-like markings decorate the back of a paradise tree snake.

❧ FLYING DRAGONS, SIZE SMALL ❧

SNAKES AREN'T THE ONLY ANIMALS sailing through the air in southeast Asian forests. Some members of the snakes' favorite food group, lizards, can fly too. Among the most skillful are the flying dragon lizards, also called Draco lizards.

Flying dragon lizards are almost invisible at rest. No longer than a school ruler, they cling to tree trunks, perfectly camouflaged by their brown and gray mottled skin. But if something disturbs a flying dragon lizard, it transforms. Leaping from the tree trunk, it snaps open a pair of brightly colored gliding wings and zips through the air with enough agility to loop around the tree trunk and land farther down, head up and alert for new dangers.

The lizard's wings are actually thin membranes of skin stretched over extra-long, hinged ribs, five to seven of them on each side of the animal's body. At rest, the ribs and membranes are folded neatly, almost invisible against the lizard's sides. When it launches into the air, the ribs open like a fan, spreading the membrane out to catch the air. The wing structures are widest behind the lizard's front legs and extend back to just in front of the hind legs. With its long tail trailing behind, the flying dragon lizard looks like a tiny, colorful kite.

Flying dragon lizards use their flying abilities for more than escape. They eat tree ants, and when they run

A flying dragon lizard looks almost like a tiny kite as it soars between trees.

short of ants on one tree, they simply glide to another tree without ever touching the ground. That saves them the extra work and danger of climbing down a tall tree, scurrying across the forest floor where plenty of predators would make a meal of a small lizard, and climbing all the way up another tree. Flying is definitely the way to go!

Flying fish leap out of the water and glide for at least 30 seconds, faster than city traffic.

FLYING FUR

THE FORESTS OF SOUTHEAST ASIA hold more unlikely fliers than anywhere else on Earth, and they aren't all reptiles. You'll also find one of the oddest mammals in the world here—the colugo (kuh-LOO-go).

Colugos are often called flying lemurs, but they're not related to lemurs. The two living species of colugo are the last of a group called Dermoptera, meaning skin-wings. One species lives only in the Philippines, and the other inhabits many of the same southeast Asian forests as the flying snakes. According to a genetic study, colugos may be the closest relatives to primates, the group that includes monkeys, apes, and us.

The Australian sugar glider, so small it could fit in a teacup, can glide with a bundle of leaves in its tail.

Cat-sized and furry, a colugo looks like an extra-large squirrel wrapped in a snuggly blanket. But when it leaps from a tree and spreads its four legs wide, the furry blanket turns into the best gliding equipment in the mammal world. A skin membrane stretches down both sides of the animal's body from chin to tail, covering all four limbs. Colugos even have webs between their fingers and toes.

During the day, colugos cling quietly and almost invisibly to trees, sometimes hanging upside down like bats. At night, they go foraging through the forest in search of leaves, shoots, buds, flowers, and fruit. They glide quietly from tree to tree in the dark, the mothers with their babies clinging to their bellies.

Because colugos are so hard to observe, we don't know a lot about them. But we do know that they're terrific gliders. In Singapore, researchers managed to attach tiny backpacks with transmitters to a handful of wild colugos. They discovered that the colugos glided from 4 to 29 times a night. Some glides were short hops from branch to branch, but one glide was estimated at 150 meters (nearly 500 feet). That's about four times as far as the Wright brothers' airplane flew in the world's first powered flight.

A colugo hangs from a tree trunk, wrapped in its furry flying membrane.

The last common ancestor of colugos and primates lived during the age of the dinosaurs.

You rarely see northern flying squirrels because they do most of their flying at night.

SECRET SQUIRREL

NOT ALL OF THE WORLD'S GLIDERS live in Asia. One of the most common squirrels in North America is a glider—and a good one—but it's rarely seen. The northern flying squirrel lives almost everywhere there are trees in North America, from North Carolina all the way north to the Yukon and Alaska. But it only comes out at night. During the day, flying squirrels stay tucked inside cozy nests, usually inside hollow trees.

Northern flying squirrels appear to be the same size as red squirrels, but only weigh about half as much. Their cousin, the southern flying squirrel, which lives in eastern North America, is even smaller —only about as big as a small mouse. Both squirrels have a furry membrane that stretches on each side of the body from front leg to back leg. A flattened tail helps them steer in the air. On a branch or on the ground, the membrane makes flying squirrels a bit clumsy. But when they launch themselves into the air and stretch out their legs, all clumsiness disappears.

At night, in the dark of the forest, their grace and skill are on display. They spend the night foraging for berries, nuts, lichens, fungi, seeds, buds, insects, and almost anything edible they come across. To move from tree to tree or from a tree to the ground, they leap from a high branch, spread their legs out, and glide, using their tails to help steer. Northern flying squirrels can weave their way among trees for as far as 50 meters (165 feet)—far enough to get from end to end of an Olympic-sized swimming pool.

RIDING a SILK BALLOON

NO MAMMAL'S GLIDING RECORD comes close to the distance a baby spider can travel through the air. Spiderlings have been known to travel more than 300 kilometers (185 miles) by air. But they don't fly or glide. They're balloonists.

At least, scientists call the method ballooning, but it's more like holding onto the end of a kite tail. On a night with a light breeze, scores of tiny spiders climb to the tops of grass stalks or twigs, raise their abdomens, and squirt out strands of silk. They're about to leave their place of birth to stake out their own web-sized patch of the planet. Each spiderling is so light that even a gentle breeze catching the silk will lift the little adventurer into the air. The spiderling drifts with the wind, dangling from its silk line, until the silk catches on

Even a spider just emerging from its egg sac, like this one, can already spin the silk it uses to build a home, catch food, or fly.

something or the wind drops and the spider floats gently to the ground in a new place.

Sometimes ballooning spiderlings travel only as far as the next grass blade, but occasionally the breeze carries them much higher and farther. Spiderlings have been spotted 4 kilometers (2.5 miles) in the air. The great naturalist Charles Darwin reported ballooning spiderlings landing on the rigging of his ship, the HMS *Beagle*, when it was 100 kilometers (60 miles) from land.

Some morning, you might walk through a meadow covered by fine threads of silk that sparkle with dew in the early light. That's all that's left of silk balloons that carried some very small animals on a great journey the night before.

The snowflakes on these berries may have carried cargoes of bacteria and other microscopic life forms to the ground.

RIDERS OF THE CLOUD

Bacteria are single-celled organisms, too small to see except through a powerful microscope. The first living things on Earth were probably bacteria, and the world—both land and ocean—is still full of them. So, it turns out, are the clouds.

Bacteria don't need to fly or glide or balloon. They simply float in air currents that can carry them to the highest clouds. Three species of bacteria have been found in the stratosphere where only the thinnest clouds form, almost 20 kilometers (12 miles) above the planet's surface.

Scientists believe some bacteria may live in the air permanently, surviving and reproducing without ever touching ground. Other bacteria come back to the earth, sometimes inside raindrops and snowflakes.

In fact, bacteria can help to create raindrops and snowflakes. The moisture in clouds clumps around particles such as dust or soot—or bacteria. If enough water clumps together, it becomes a raindrop. Or, if conditions are right, ice crystals form and snowflakes fall. In one study of snowflakes, up to 85 percent of the flakes in some samples had bacteria at their centers. So people who love skiing or snowboarding or snowball fights can thank bacteria for their winter fun.

> Bacteria are tiny scraps of life, so small you can only see them through a microscope. Some of them cause diseases, but most are harmless or even helpful to people.

5 DOWN IN THE DARK

~ LIVING in the DARK ~

MOST HUMANS DEPEND SO MUCH ON SIGHT that it's hard to imagine living in complete darkness. And we need light for more than seeing. Our bodies need sunlight to function properly, and without it, we get sick.

But some animals spend their entire lives in the dark, in places where life seems impossible. Others hide from light and are active only during the dark hours. And they all survive just fine.

Animals that live in the dark have to solve some problems. For example, how do you find your way around? When there isn't much light, how do you see where you're going? And if you're flying or running or swimming through darkness, how do you avoid crashing into things?

Food is another problem. How do you find dinner in the dark?

And how do you meet friends and avoid enemies?

Bats are well known for living and hunting in the dark. But they're not the only animals more comfortable out of the light.

61

Oilbirds live in caves and can find their way around by sound, much as bats do.

TICK-TOCK in the DARK

HEARING AN ANIMAL MOVING AROUND in the dark isn't too surprising. Plenty of small mammals come out at night because they're safer from big animals. Raccoons raid garbage cans in the dark or feel about in streams for tasty water creatures. And if you hear clicking sounds at night and something flutters overhead, you would—quite sensibly—think, "Bat!"

But if you happened to be near the Guacharo (GWA-cha-row) Caves in Venezuela, you could be wrong. In 1799, a group of local people took the famous German naturalist Alexander von Humboldt to the caves to show him something he'd never seen before—birds that live deep in caves and find their way around like bats. And tourists have been coming to see them ever since.

Oilbirds are about the size of crows, with reddish-brown feathers and scattered, black-rimmed white dots. The Guacharo Caves are the most famous oilbird caves, but these birds are found in other large caves from Costa Rica through northern South America. During the day, they roost quietly on ledges inside the caves. In the evening, as darkness thickens, the oilbirds come to life. They begin by making a racket, a combination of squawks and clicks, as they greet each other, stretch their wings, and then set out for the night's work, flying skillfully through the black cave.

Super-fast bursts of clicks are the birds' way of navigating. Like bats, they listen for the echo of the clicks in order to avoid obstacles. Their brains sort the information from the echoes so quickly that oilbirds can weave their way through the cave and out its entrance without running into the walls or each other.

Once they're in the open, they navigate both by sight and smell. Their sense of smell leads them to their preferred food, fruit. Oilbirds eat about two dozen kinds of fruit, but their favorite is the fruit of oil palms, which people also harvest to make palm oil. The birds hover beside a tree and pluck the plum-sized fruit with their hooked beaks, gulping it down whole. They'll digest it later—and vomit up the pits—back in the dark comfort of their cave.

This barn owl uses both sound and sight to hunt at night.

Before dawn, large flocks of oilbirds gather and head to their caves. They squawk loudly as they pass through the entrance and then click their way through the darkness to their roosting sites.

❧ FOREVER in DARKNESS ❧

PART-TIME CAVE-DWELLERS like oilbirds still experience some light. Even a moonless night isn't as dark as the deep caves of the world, places where no light reaches at all. Few animals can survive there, and not only because of the darkness. There's not much to eat in deep caves.

You have to be tough to live in such a place. And the olm, despite its delicate appearance, is tough.

The olm is a salamander found in limestone caverns along the north-central coast of the Mediterranean Sea. About as long as a dinner knife and almost snakelike, it has four short legs and pink external gills on each side of its head. Olms live in underground streams and in the water running through dark, damp passages far below Earth's surface. Over many generations, olms have changed to suit their homes.

The most noticeable change is their color. Most olms never experience light in their entire lives, so they don't need colored pigment in their skins to protect them from the sun. Their skin is pale, translucent, and pinkish, most of its color from blood running through vessels just beneath the skin.

The lack of light also means they don't really need to see, so their eyes have deteriorated. The eyes can still sense light, but that's all. They're permanently covered by a layer of skin.

This tiny olm lives its whole life in the darkness of a huge cave in eastern Europe.

That doesn't mean that olms are helpless. They've made up for lack of sight by developing other senses. They're experts at using taste, smell, hearing, and even electric currents to detect edible tidbits—tiny invertebrates and bits of decaying matter—swept into the caves by water draining from the surface, far above.

And they've developed an even more important ability for living in barren underground depths. They stuff themselves with food when they can, but they can live at least 10 years without eating at all. No one knows how long they can live altogether, but it might be more than a century.

> Found only in a tiny corner of Slovenia, the extremely rare black olm has working eyes.

A CAVE FULL of STARS

THE WAITOMO RIVER IN NEW ZEALAND winds through huge caves formed more than 30 million years ago. You can squeeze into a wet-suit, strap on a headlamp, and float through the cave system on an inner tube—or, if you're feeling less adventurous, ride in a boat.

However you travel, all the lights will be turned off in one huge cavern. As you bob gently on the slow-moving river, your eyes adjusting to the darkness, you realize that the cavern isn't completely dark. Above you, its roof is dotted with points of light like a starry night sky. But the lights are bluish, and hang in garlands and streamers from the cavern ceiling.

What you're seeing is thousands of tiny traps that attract insects with their glowing light. They're the work of Waitomo glowworms, the larvae of a fly called a fungus gnat (pronounced nat). Although fungus gnats live throughout the world, only four species—all in New Zealand or Australia—have larvae that glow.

The Waitomo glowworms gather in dark places and spin silken traps. First, the worm makes a cozy tube of mucus produced from its anus, and attaches both ends of the tube to the cavern roof. Then it spins fine silk threads that dangle straight down, barely moving in the still cave air. Dotted along the dangling threads and on the tube itself are drops of glue-like mucus. The mucus reacts with the air by glowing blue, an effect called bioluminescence, and the glow attracts insects that live in the cave or blunder into it by accident.

When an insect bumps into a strand of silk, the glue traps it, and its struggles alert the glowworm. The glowworm hauls in the thread and eats the captive insect. But what if the cave doesn't provide enough flies and other creatures to feed its thousands of glowworms? No problem. They eat each other. Only one glowworm in ten survives to become an adult fungus gnat. The adults' lives are short, just long enough to mate and lay the eggs that will produce another generation of glowworms.

A LIFE in EARTH

EARTHWORMS SPEND THEIR LIVES in the dark, munching their way through organic matter in the ground and turning it into soil. They're almost everywhere, so there's nothing unexpected about turning up a squirmy pink-brown worm when you dig in the garden or poke through loose dirt in a park.

But how about an earthworm thicker than a man's finger and at least as long as his belt? Now that's unexpected! That, in fact, is the giant Gippsland earthworm.

The worm gets its name from the only place it lives, a river valley in the Gippsland region of southern Australia. It looks like the worms you turn up in the garden, only much, much bigger. It's hard to say exactly how much bigger, since earthworms can stretch out long or scrunch up short. While the average giant worm is about belt-length, it could be twice that long when stretched.

The giant Gippsland earthworm is fragile and rarely seen above ground.

Stretching a Gippsland earthworm out to measure it is, however, a bad idea. Despite their size, the worms are extremely fragile and likely to break if stretched. Even slight bruising can kill them.

Giant Gippsland earthworms are designed for one thing only—to spend their lives in dark tunnels in the ground, eating. Their tunnels are large, about as thick across as a garden hose, and can go 2 meters (6 feet) down into the ground. Unlike most earthworms, the Gippsland earthworm builds a network of permanent tunnels and burrows. The worms don't come to the surface even to deposit their eggs or to poop, as most earthworms do. That makes them hard to study, and scientists still don't know much about their lives down there in the dark.

It's possible to hear them, though. If you stamp hard on the ground in worm territory, especially when the ground is damp, you're likely to hear a gurgling sound coming from below. That's the sound of a giant Gippsland earthworm retreating down its watery tunnel to escape the noisy surface-dweller.

✄ EYEING UP the PREY ✄

NEAR ITS SURFACE, the ocean is flooded with light, but if you dive down, light soon fades and eventually disappears. The depths of the ocean are as dark as any cave. That's not where you'd expect to find a fish that's best known for its eyes. Yet that's where the barreleye lives, hanging almost motionless in the water about 700 meters (2300 feet) below the surface, where only the faintest glow of sunlight reaches.

The barreleye, no larger than a milk carton, has puzzled scientists for more than 60 years. Despite living in the dark, the barreleye has spectacular eyes. They're large and tube-shaped. That's a great design for gathering light, but it's like looking through a pair of

Protected by a transparent shield, the barreleye's strange eyes can swivel to look up through the top of its head or straight ahead.

toilet paper rolls. The fish should be able to see only what is directly in front of its eyes.

Although barreleyes have been found in the Atlantic, Pacific, and Indian oceans, until recently, scientists had only seen fish that were caught in fishing nets. Judging by those dead and damaged specimens, it appeared that the fish's tubular eyes pointed straight upward, so it looked directly above its head. It wouldn't be able to see what it was eating or where it was going.

The barreleye's peculiar eyes remained a puzzle until researchers used a remotely operated camera to observe live barreleyes, off the coast of California. What they saw amazed them.

The barreleyes floated almost motionless in the water, with their eyes pointed straight up. But the eyes were protected behind a transparent shield, like the mask on a motorcycle helmet, so fragile that

Sunlight fades away rapidly as you go deeper in the ocean.

it had not survived on the fish caught in nets. Then they saw a fish point its head toward the surface. In the fluid-filled cavity behind the transparent shield, the fish's eyes swiveled forward so that it was looking straight out over its mouth. When the fish went back to a horizontal position, the eyes swiveled back to look through the clear shield on top of its head.

Scientists are still trying to figure out why the fish's eyes work like this. They think the sensitive eyes might point upward so that the barreleye can spot prey such as jellyfish outlined by the faint glow of light from above. Then, when it sees a potential meal, the eyes rotate into the forward position so the fish can see what it's hunting.

BOMB-THROWING WORMS

You wouldn't expect to find much almost 4 kilometers (2.5 miles) beneath the surface of the ocean. It's cold down there, and far beyond the reach of sunlight.

You certainly wouldn't expect to find lively glow-in-the-dark worms with transparent bodies and dozens of feathery paddle-like bristles propelling them through the water. And the last thing you'd expect is to watch some of those worms, when disturbed, toss out glowing balls of bioluminescent material like miniature bombs.

Nevertheless, that's what a group of American biologists found near the seabed off the west coast of the United States. The researchers call them Swima worms and have identified several species so far. Five of those species drop the luminescent "bombs" when disturbed.

Each worm appears to have about eight bombs, and it might drop one or two when nudged or threatened. As soon as they're released, the tiny spheres start glowing bright green, distracting the attacker—and allowing the worm to swim safely away. Over time, it will grow a new set of light bombs.

Tiny Swima worms fire off light bombs to escape from predators.

6

ICE IS NICE

❧ LIVING *in the* COLD ❧

WHEN IT GETS COLD OUTSIDE, many animals get going. They migrate to warmer places or snuggle down in dens to hibernate. Humans dig out their winter clothes and light a fire or turn on a furnace.

Cold can be a danger for animals. Mammals and birds have to keep their body temperatures fairly high, near the temperature of a hot summer's day, or they'll die. Other animals, such as insects and amphibians, have body temperatures controlled by their surroundings, but if the temperature around them gets too low, they'll also die.

So, one big problem animals have to solve in cold places is finding ways to protect their bodies from the chill.

Another problem is finding food. In winter, many animals move away, plants stop growing, leaves disappear from

Ice and cold mean comfort to a polar bear.

trees, water freezes, and snow covers the ground. There's not nearly as much food around as there is in summer, and what remains is often hidden from sight.

But not everyone retreats from the cold. Some animals adjust the way they live, others barely notice it, and still others are right at home.

Japanese macaques warm up in winter by soaking in a hot spring.

⌘ A COZY WHITE BLANKET ⌘

WHEN YOU LOOK AT A SNOW-COVERED FIELD or the forest floor in the dead of winter, they look, well, dead. At most, you might see a few tracks from a passing rabbit or the neighbor's dog. But looks can be deceiving, and that's definitely true when it comes to snow cover. Whole communities exist on, in, and under the snow, taking advantage of snow's special qualities.

If you could look at a cross-section of the snow cover, from the surface to the ground, you'd find it's not all one fluffy mass. Layers are created by different snowfalls or by ice where surface snow melted and then froze again. And at the bottom is the most important place of all—the subnivean space.

Snow is surprisingly good at protecting the ground from extreme winter temperatures. It might be well below freezing in the air above, but the ground beneath the snow is warmer, changing the snowflakes into large, loosely packed crystals. In places, the snow even shrinks away from the ground. This layer of open air and large, loose crystals is called the subnivean ("under snow") space, and it's where northern red-backed voles spend the winter.

When winter comes, this northern red-backed vole will still wander the forest floor in search of blueberries—underneath a blanket of snow.

Red-backed voles look like mice with short tails and rusty-colored fur on their backs. They live in the forests, tundras, and bogs of North America, Europe, and Asia. In summer, they scurry about, eating grass, seeds, fruit, lichens, insects, and almost anything else they come across. In southern regions, where winters are warm, voles carry on scurrying and eating—and making baby voles—all year round. In northern regions, where winter means months of cold and snow, red-backed voles make some adjustments.

All voles store food, but northern red-backed voles are the champions. In one summer, a single vole can sock away as much as 3 kilograms (6.5 pounds) of food to help it through the winter. Once winter arrives, northern voles make another adjustment. They keep right on scurrying and eating, but they do it under the snow. The voles munch on flattened grasses or burrow up through the snow until they find a layer covered with seeds, but they depend mainly on the food they stashed over the summer.

And they share. In summer, female voles establish territories and defend them against other females, while the males look for food and for mates. In winter, however, voles don't waste energy fighting each other. Instead, whole groups huddle together for warmth when they're not out searching for food.

Winter life for voles is not only about eating and snuggling. Danger lurks in their dark tunnels. Weasels and tiny, fierce shrews travel the tunnels too, and coyotes and owls hunt from above. Even humans are a problem. Ski trails and snow machine tracks compress the subnivean space, forcing tunnel-dwellers to dash across open snow where owls and other predators—or the cold itself—can kill them.

Still, the under-snow world is no more dangerous than the summer world for voles, and can be almost as comfortable.

Coyotes listen for the sounds of animals moving under the snow and catch them by pouncing to break through the crust.

FEATHERS are not ENOUGH

WHILE SOME ANIMALS live under the snow all winter, other creatures use the insulating blanket of snow temporarily. If you could look beneath the snow on a cold night, you might come across the unexpected sight of a fairly large bird snuggled into a cave well under the surface.

Grouse and ptarmigan are common residents in snowy landscapes of the northern hemisphere. These plump birds, about the size of a small chicken, make good eating for lynx, coyotes, and other wild hunters, as well as humans. The birds spend their days above the snow, eating buds and evergreen needles, protected by thick coats of insulating feathers. Ptarmigan even have feathered feet that help them walk across the snow without sinking in.

However, on cold winter nights, extra protection is welcome. Both grouse and ptarmigan will dive into fluffy snow and use their wings and feet to swim deeper, kicking up snow behind them as they go. Once they're deep enough that the cold air from above can't reach them, they wriggle around a bit to make a den. The snow they kicked back blocks drafts from the entrance. And there they stay all night, safely protected by a warm blanket of snow. During a cold snap, some birds even spend several days and nights in a row under the snow, snug in their cozy white nests.

A white-tailed ptarmigan snuggles down in a comfortable hole in the snow.

Glacier ice worms hide from the sun during the day and come out in the evening.

ICE-WRIGGLERS

SNOW-COVERED GLACIERS look even more bleak and lifeless than snow-covered fields and forests. You wouldn't expect to find much life high in the mountains where the snow and ice of centuries fill entire valleys. And probably the last thing you'd expect is a worm.

But worms live even there. On mountain glaciers along the western coast of North America, from Oregon to southern Alaska, you can find tiny worms called glacier ice worms. Their scientific name is *Mesenchytraeus solifugus* (mez-en-kih-TRAY-us saw-lih-FEW-gus), and they're so small that three or four of them could fit end to end under their name. When they come to the surface, they look like bits of black string discarded on the snow.

Like their larger relatives the earthworms, glacier ice worms don't like direct sunlight. They come to the surface in the evening to graze on snow algae and microscopic organisms. When dawn comes, they burrow far beneath the snow, or retreat to meltwater pools and streams where the water protects them from sunlight.

The cold doesn't seem to bother them. Like many cold-climate organisms, the glacier ice worm has a protein in its cells that acts like antifreeze and prevents the cells from freezing as the temperature drops. In a more unusual adaptation, the glacier ice worm's metabolism speeds up as the temperature gets colder—the opposite of most animals, including most worms.

Glacier ice worms have been found only where permanent ice lies underneath the snow cover. But there, they can be plentiful. A group of researchers counting glacier ice worms in Washington State estimated that one glacier was home to about seven billion ice worms. That's more than the world population of humans.

So think of glacier ice worms the next time someone talks about water as pure as a mountain glacier!

LIFE in a FROZEN MUSHROOM

IF YOU'RE GOING TO LOOK for something as unexpected as ice worms, at least glaciers are a logical place to look. You probably wouldn't look for them at the bottom of a warm ocean. But that, surprisingly, would be a mistake.

Two scientists in a research submarine dove to the bottom of the Gulf of Mexico to explore the sea floor. There, 700 meters (almost 2300 feet) below the surface, the water is much colder. And there, they found a mushroom-shaped mound of methane ice as big as a king-sized bed, pushing up through the bottom sediments. Methane ice sometimes forms where methane gas is seeping from beneath the sea floor, and the Gulf of Mexico is one of the few places where it pushes above the sediment.

This lump of frozen methane deep in the Gulf of Mexico is riddled with methane ice worms.

But the scientists found more than ice. The ice mound was riddled with holes, and in each hole was a flat, pinkish worm with masses of feathery white bristles. The largest was no longer than your little finger. They were bristle worms, a kind of marine worm distantly related to glacier ice worms. The scientists calculated that there were thousands in that single piece of ice.

Since that discovery, more worm-infested blocks of methane ice have been found in the Gulf of Mexico. The worms seem to eat bacteria that grow on the ice and may help break the ice down, but what else they might eat or do has yet to be discovered.

When they're small, krill often hide in the cracks and pores on the underside of antarctic sea ice.

MEALS under ICE

BETWEEN THE GLACIERS high in the mountains and the methane ice deep in the oceans, there's another kind of ice—sea ice. It floats on the polar oceans, growing in winter and shrinking in summer. A few large animals, such as polar bears in the Arctic and penguins in Antarctica, spend time on the ice surface. Fish and whales live underneath it. But the ice itself looks like a white desert, empty of life.

Seen from below, however, sea ice is anything but empty. It's a combination of jungle, cave system, meadow, and hunting ground. Super-salty water—too salty to freeze—creates pores and tunnels, and cold-adapted algae grow across the ice's underside and up into the pores. Tiny organisms graze on the algae, and other small creatures graze on them. Miniature worms squeeze through the pores, eating anything they come across.

In the ocean around Antarctica, the underside of sea ice is also a nursery for one of the most important animals in the southern ocean—the antarctic krill. The little shrimplike crustaceans don't look important. However, without them, much larger animals would starve. They're a vital food source for squid, penguins, and many seals and whales. In fact, the largest animal the world has ever known, the blue whale, eats nothing but krill.

A humpback whale lunges through the surface, gulping in water and sea creatures, such as krill, in one huge mouthful. The gulls and shearwaters are hoping for leftovers.

Krill may be important to a lot of sea animals, but sea ice is vital to antarctic krill. Krill, like shrimp, filter bits of food out of the sea water around them. But antarctic krill have special adaptations for living with sea ice. They scrape food off the ice itself like tiny backhoes, using rows of rakelike projections on the tips of their

A blue whale can gulp down thousands of krill in a single mouthful.

legs. This adaptation means that immature krill can hang around the underside of the sea ice and scrape algae, bacteria, and other organisms from the ice surface, gobbling up almost half their body weight in a day. When predators threaten, the krill retreat into the safety of the ice pores.

Adult krill hang around under the sea ice too, even when they're too big to hide in its pores. They still eat algae and bacteria, but they also eat smaller crustaceans. And they grow and multiply. Krill are so good at eating and growing and multiplying—and the antarctic sea ice is such a rich source of food for them—that the krill form huge swarms, big enough to feed a giant whale. Altogether, those swarms weigh about 1.5 billion tonnes. That's roughly three times the total weight of all the people on Earth.

The food and shelter offered by the sea ice are so important to antarctic krill that their numbers plummet if the amount of sea ice shrinks. And fewer krill means starvation for many of the animals that depend on them.

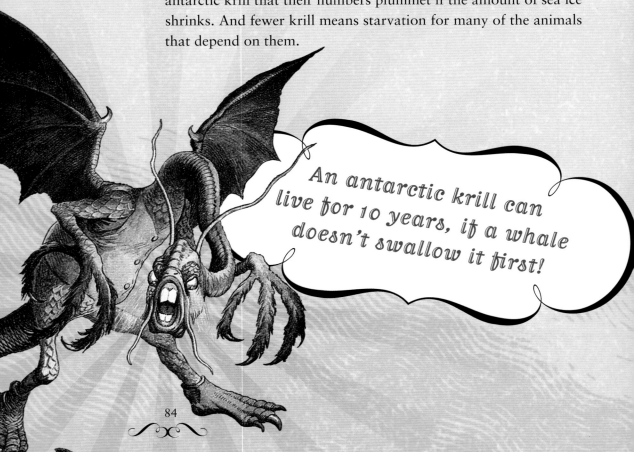

An antarctic krill can live for 10 years, if a whale doesn't swallow it first!

BONE-DEEP CHANGE

Shrews are tiny, mouselike insect-eaters, most no bigger than a grown-up's thumb. They're found in most parts of the world, from the tropics to the northern tundra. And that's surprising.

Shrews burn energy at an extremely high rate. A shrew's heart might beat 1200 times a minute, the same as a humming-bird's. Even in warm weather, a shrew has to hunt day and night just to stay alive, so how can it survive the freezing cold of winter?

In winter, northern shrews stay under the snow, poking through leaf litter for insect pupae and eggs or hunting through tunnels for the small animals that dug them. Between hunting trips, they retreat into nests and curl up to stay warm. The cold of the world above the snow would kill them in minutes.

Amazingly, northern shrews change their bodies as well as their behavior when the temperature drops. They get smaller—and not just skinnier. Their body weight goes down by as much as a third, their brains and internal organs shrink, their skulls change shape, and their spines get shorter. A smaller body needs less food to fuel it, and because there's less body surface, the shrew's hairs are closer together for better insulation.

To survive the cold of winter, shrews make many changes—some of them truly bone-deep.

The tiny shrew is a fierce hunter, summer and winter.

APPENDIX:
SCIENTIFIC NAMES OF FEATURED ANIMALS

WATER
American dipper – *Cinclus mexicanus*
star-nosed mole – *Condylura cristata*
water spider – *Argyroneta aquatica*
sea skater – *Halobates* (several species)
yellow-bellied sea snake – *Pelamis platurus*
water chevrotain – *Hyemoschus aquaticus*

LAND
common woodlouse – *Porcellio laevis*
eel catfish – *Channallabes apus*
freshwater eel – many species
mudskipper – 36 species (Gobiidae family)
burrowing owl – *Athene cunicularia*
kakapo – *Strigops habroptila*
mangrove killifish – *Kryptolebias marmoratus*

DESERT
fairy shrimp – about 300 species
water-holding frog – *Cyclorana platycephala*
Namaqua sandgrouse – *Pterocles namaqua*
white-tailed antelope ground squirrel – *Ammospermophilus
    leucurus*
desert tortoise – *Gopherus agassizii*
naked mole rat – *Heterocephalus glaber*

AIR

paradise tree snake – *Chrysopelea paradisi*

flying dragon lizard – *Draco* (more than 40 species)

colugo – *Cynocephalus volans* and *Galeopterus variegatus*

northern and southern flying squirrel – *Glaucomys sabrinus* and *Glaucomys volans*

ballooning spider – many species

airborne bacteria – many species

DARK

oilbird – *Steatornis caripensis*

olm – *Proteus anguinus*

Waitomo glowworm/fungus gnat – *Arachnocampa luminosa*

giant Gippsland earthworm – *Megascolides australis*

barreleye – *Macropinna microstoma*

bomb-throwing worm – *Swima* (several species, most still unnamed)

COLD

northern red-backed vole – *Myodes rutilus,* also called *Clethrionomys rutilus*

grouse – several species

ptarmigan – several species

glacier ice worm – *Mesenchytraeus solifugus*

methane ice worm – *Hesiocaeca methanicola*

antarctic krill – *Euphausia superba*

northern shrew – several species (Soricidae family)

FURTHER READING

Barnhill, Kelly Regan. *Animals with No Eyes: Cave Adaptation.* Mankato, MN: Capstone Press, 2008.

Bayrock, Fiona. *Bubble Homes and Fish Farts.* Watertown, MA: Charlesbridge, 2009.

Breidahl, Harry. *Extremophiles: Life in Extreme Environments.* Broomall, PA: Chelsea House, 2002.

Conlan, Kathy. *Under the Ice.* Toronto: Kids Can Press, 2002.

Davies, Nicola. *Extreme Animals: The Toughest Creatures on Earth.* Cambridge, MA: Candlewick Press, reprint 2009.

Dixon, Norma. *Lowdown on Earthworms.* Markham, ON, and Allston, MA: Fitzhenry and Whiteside, 2005.

Kelsey, Elin. *Strange New Species: Astonishing Discoveries of Life on Earth.* Toronto: Maple Tree Press, 2005.

Latta, Sara L. *The Good, the Bad, the Slimy: The Secret Life of Microbes.* Berkeley Heights, NJ: Enslow, 2006.

Lindop, Laurie. *Cave Sleuths.* Minneapolis, MN: Twenty-First Century Books, 2006.

McGhee, Karen, and George McKay. *National Geographic Encyclopedia of Animals.* Des Moines, IA: National Geographic Children's Books, 2006.

Piper, Ross. *Extraordinary Animals: An Encyclopedia of Curious and Unusual Animals.* Westport, CT and London: Greenwood Press, 2007.

Rosenberg, Pam. *Ack! Icky, Sticky, Gross Stuff Underground.* Mankato, MN: Child's World, 2008.

SELECTED BIBLIOGRAPHY

Alderton, David. *Rodents of the World*. London: Blandford, 1999.

Andersen, Nils M. "*Halobates*—Oceanic Insects." Website copyright N. M. Andersen and Zoological Museum, University of Copenhagen, 2001. Retrieved July 27, 2009, from http://www.zmuc.dk/EntoWeb/Halotab1.htm.

Attenborough, D. *Life in the Undergrowth*. Princeton and Oxford: Princeton University Press, 2005.

———. *The Life of Birds*. Princeton: Princeton University Press, 1998.

Badger, D. *Lizards: A Natural History of Some Uncommon Creatures— Extraordinary Chameleons, Iguanas, Geckos, and More*. Stillwater, MN: Voyageur Press, 2002.

Baker, Nick. "Olm (*Proteus anguinus*)." EDGE: Amphibian Species Information. Retrieved Oct. 1, 2009, from http://www.edgeofexistence.org/amphibians/ species_info.php?id=563

Bastedo, J. *Falling for Snow*. Calgary: Red Deer Press, 2003.

BirdLife International. "Species factsheet: *Steatornis caripensis* (2009)." Retrieved Sept. 30, 2009, from http://www.birdlife.org.

Black, Scott and Alan Fehr, eds. *Natural History of the Western Arctic*. Inuvik, NT: Western Arctic Handbook Committee, 2002.

Bouglouan, Nicole. "Oilbird." Retrieved Sept. 30, 2009, from http://www. oiseaux-birds.com/card-oilbird.html.

Catania, Kenneth C. "Underwater 'Sniffing' by Semi-aquatic Mammals." *Nature* 444 (Dec. 28, 2006): 1024–25.

———. "Star-nosed moles." *Current Biology* 15.21 (Nov. 8, 2005): 863–64.

Christner, Brent C., Cindy E. Morris, Christine M. Foreman, Rongman Cai, and David C. Sands. "Ubiquity of Biological Ice Nucleators in Snowfall." *Science* 319 (Feb. 29, 2008): 1214.

Croke, Vicki. "Exposed: The Strange and Hidden Lives of Naked Mole-rats." *National Wildlife* 37.5 (Aug./Sept. 1999): 16–17.

Dolgin, Elie. "The Swamp Fish that Loves to Live in Trees." *New Scientist* 2626 (Oct. 19, 2007). Retrieved Dec. 22, 2009, from http://www.newscientist. com/article/mg19626264.400-the-swamp-fish-that-loves-to-live-in-trees. html.

"Egg Sacs, Spiderlings and Dispersal." Australian Museum (Mar. 6, 2009). Retrieved Sept. 18, 2009, from http://australianmuseum.net.au/Egg-sacs- spiderlings-and-dispersal.

"Facts about the American Eel." U.S. Fish & Wildlife Service (April 2005). Retrieved Sept. 24, 2009, from http://www.fws.gov/northeast/AmEel/facts. html.

Fisher C.R., I.R. MacDonald, R. Sassen, C.M. Young, S.A. Macko, S. Hourdez, R.S. Carney, S. Joye, and E. McMullin. "Methane Ice Worms: *Hesiocaeca methanicola* Colonizing Fossil Fuel Reserves." *Naturwissenschaften* 87.4 (April 2000):184–87.

Flying Snake. 1999–2005. Retrieved September 29, 2009, from http://www.flyingsnake.org.

"Giant Gippsland Earthworm." *Animal Aqua* (Dec. 16, 2006). Retrieved Sept. 30, 2009, from http://www.animalaqua.com/giant-gippsland-earthworm.

Gill, Victoria. "Glowing 'Bomber Worms' Discovered." *BBC NEWS, Science & Environment* (Aug. 21, 2009). Retrieved Sept. 30, 2009, from http://news.bbc.co.uk/2/hi/science/nature/8210645.stm

Hainsworth, F. Reed. "Optimal Body Temperatures with Shuttling: Desert Antelope Ground Squirrels. *Animal Behaviour* 49 (1995): 107–16.

Hartzell, Paula L., Jefferson V. Nghiem, Kristina J. Richio, and Daniel H. Shain. "Distribution and Phylogeny of Glacier Ice Worms (*Mesenchytraeus solifugus* and *Mesenchytraeus solifugus rainierensis*)." *Canadian Journal of Zoology* 83 (2005): 1206–13.

Hattam, Jennifer. "I Grab the Feet of the Person Behind Me, Then Swing My Own Legs onto the Inner Tube. *Sierra* 94. 3 (May/June 2009): 26–27.

Haug, E.A., B.A. Millsap, and M.S. Martell. "Burrowing Owl." In A. Poole and F. Gill (eds.). *The Birds of North America* 61 (1993): 1–19.

Henry, J. David. *Canada's Boreal Forest*. Washington and London: Smithsonian Institution Press, 2002.

Higgins, P.J., senior ed. *Handbook of Australian, New Zealand and Antarctic Birds, vol. 4: Parrots to Dollarbird*. Oxford: Oxford University Press, 1999.

Hogarth, P. J. *The Biology of Mangroves*. Oxford: Oxford University Press, 1999.

Hooper, Rowan. "Bacteria Make Snow to Get Back Home." *New Scientist* 2646 (Mar. 8, 2008). Retrieved Dec. 22, 2009, from http://www.newscientist.com/article/mg19726464.500-airborne-bacteria-make-snow-to-get-back-home.html.

Ishimatsu, Atsushi, Yu Yoshida, Naoko Itoki, Tatsusuke Takeda, Heather J. Lee, and Jeffrey B. Graham. "Mudskippers Brood their Eggs in Air but Submerge Them for Hatching." *The Journal of Experimental Biology* 210 (2007): 3946–54.

Jones, H., J. Pomeroy, D. Walker, and R. Hoham, eds. *Snow Ecology: An Interdisciplinary Examination of Snow-covered Ecosystems*. Cambridge, UK: Cambridge University Press, 2001.

Mackinnon, J., et al. *Borneo*. Amsterdam: Time-Life International (Nederland) B.V., 1975.

Mattison, C. *300 Frogs: A Visual Reference to Frogs and Toads from Around the World*. Buffalo: Firefly Books, 2007.

Mehta, Aalok (Nov 6, 2007). "Fish Lives in Logs, Breathing Air, for Months at a Time." *National Geographic News*. Retrieved Sept. 26, 2009, from http://news.nationalgeographic.com/news/pf/93334015.html.

Mohr, C.E., and T.L. Poulson. *The Life of the Cave*. New York: McGraw-Hill, 1966.

Morelle, Rebecca. "African Fish Leaps for Land Bugs." *BBC News* (Apr. 12, 2006). Retrieved Feb. 21, 2009, from http://news.bbc.co.uk/go/pr/fr/-/2/hi/science/nature/4902784.stm.

"Mouse-deer Swims Underwater to Escape Predators. *Fish and Aquatic News* (July 8, 2009). Retrieved Sept. 20, 2009, from http://www.aquaticcommunity.com/news/lib/391.

"Namaqua Sandgrouse." *Encounter South Africa Magazine* (online). Retrieved Sept. 28, 2009, from http://www.encounter.co.za/article/127.html.

North Cascades Glacier Ice Worm research. North Cascade Glacier Climate Project. Nichols College, Dudley, MA. Retrieved Oct. 1, 2009, from http://www.nichols.edu/departments/glacier/iceworm.htm.

Osborne, Tim. "Voles." Wildlife Notebook Series (1994). Alaska Department of Fish and Game. Retrieved Oct. 2, 2009, from http://www.adfg.state.ak.us/pubs/notebook/smgame/voles.php.

Pain, Stephanie. "Lair of the Ice Worms." *New Scientist* 2094 (Aug. 9, 1997). Retrieved Dec. 22, 2009, from http://www.newscientist.com/article/mg15520943.900-lair-of-the-ice-worms.html.

Pollard, Simon. "Queens of the Desert." *Nature Australia* 28.2 (spring 2004): 72–73.

———. "Squirming Fleshy Tentacles of Doom." *Nature Australia* 28.7 (summer 2005/2006): 68–69.

Pruitt, W.O.J. *Wild Harmony: Animals of the North*. Vancouver: Douglas & McIntyre, 1967.

"Researchers Solve Mystery of Deep-sea Fish with Tubular Eyes and Transparent Head." Monterey Bay Aquarium Research Institute news release (Feb. 23, 2009). Retrieved Sept. 30, 2009, from http://www.mbari.org/news/news_releases/2009/barreleye/barreleye.html.

Runyan, Curtis. "Underwater Deer: Researchers Observe a New Behavior in Borneo." *Nature Conservancy Magazine* (spring 2009). Retrieved Sept. 20, 2009, from http://www.nature.org/magazine/spring2009/issues/art27311.html.

Sinclair, Pamela H., Wendy A. Nixon, Cameron D. Eckert, and Nancy L. Hughes, eds. *Birds of the Yukon Territory*. Vancouver: UBC Press, 2003.

Smith, Matthew D., and Courtney J. Conway. "Use of Mammal Manure by Nesting Burrowing Owls: A Test of Four Functional Hypotheses. *Animal Behaviour* 73 (2007): 65–73.

Snakes: A Natural History. New York: Sterling, 1994.

Taylor, Scott D., Bruce J. Turner, William P. Davis, and Ben B. Chapman. "A Novel Terrestrial Fish Habitat inside Emergent Logs." *The American Naturalist* 171.2 (Feb. 2008): 263–66.

Thomas, David N. *Frozen Oceans: The Floating World of Pack Ice*. London: Firefly Books, 2004.

Turbak, Gary. "The Bird that Flies through Water." *National Wildlife* 38.4 (June/July 2000): 28–32.

Van Praagh, B.D. "Giant Gippsland Earthworm: 'Nature's Plough.'" Land for Wildlife Notes (July 1999). State of Victoria, Department of Natural Resources and Environment. Retrieved Sept. 30, 2009, from http://www.dpi.vic.gov.au/DPI/nreninf.nsf/9e58661e880ba9e44a256c640023eb2e/a40d42cb19bd6e98ca256e7d0020589b/$FILE/ATTE04DN/LW0011.pdf.

Van Wassenbergh, Sam, Anthony Herrel, Dominique Adriaens, Frank Huysentruyt, Stijn Devaere, and Peter Aerts. "A Catfish That Can Strike its Prey on Land." *Nature* 440 (April 2006): 881.

"Water-holding Frog." Frogwatch. Western Australian Museum. Retrieved Sept. 28, 2009, from http://frogwatch.museum.wa.gov.au/AridZone/649.aspx.

Woods, S.E., Jr. *The Squirrels of Canada*. Ottawa: National Museums of Canada, 1980.

INDEX

ACKNOWLEDGMENTS

DOING THE RESEARCH FOR THIS BOOK led me to animals even stranger than I had imagined—and I can imagine some pretty strange animals! My thanks to all the researchers who are just as entranced by the natural world as I am and who spend so much time trying to learn more about it. And special appreciation to staff at the Canadian Museum of Nature who, busy as they are, gave me access to both their library and their formidable expertise.

In particular, I'd like to thank the following people who read the full manuscript in search of errors: Joan Eamer, Ted Osmond-Jones, Susan Thompson, and Syd Cannings.

I'd also like to thank the following people who checked portions of the manuscript: Scott Gilbert, Pam Sinclair, Erik Meijaard, Andrew Hearn, Ken Catania, Ferne Mackenzie, Emma Neill, Jake Socha, Patricia A. Wright, Chuck Fisher, Deirdre Vercoe, Mauri Pelto, Will Duckworth, Karen Osborn, Ira Rubinoff, Jeff Graham, and Jonathan Murray.

They all did their best to make the science accurate. Any errors that remain are mine, not theirs.

PHOTO CREDITS

ABOUT THE AUTHOR

CLAIRE EAMER lives in the Yukon in northern Canada and writes about science for both kids and adults. She discovered long ago that writing about science allowed her to ask as many questions as she wanted—and she loves asking questions. When not asking questions or writing about the answers, Claire likes traveling, reading, and poking around in museums in search of more questions and answers.